I0481502

Litecoin:

Best Strategies for Investing

and Profiting From Litecoin

MARK CLARKSON

Table of Contents

Introduction

Congratulations on purchasing *Litecoin: Best Strategies for Investing and Profiting From Litecoin* and thank you for doing so.

By now, you've already heard about the importance of cryptocurrencies and why they are so important to our technological future. The concept of decentralization is definitely capturing the interests of people everywhere. Names like Bitcoin and Ethereum, are frequently on the tips of the tongues of millions of people.

If you are like most, the pull to be a part of this revolutionary change is very powerful. Evidence of this is clear when you look at the numbers of the top currencies on the market as they continue to rise. As these market leaders continue to skyrocket at rates one might have never imagined, the names of other altcoins are also becoming familiar.

One of those coins, Litecoin, is now pushing its way to the forefront and is looking to be rapidly coming up on the heels of his big brother. This book was created to help many to get to know Litecoin the way that millions have come to know Bitcoin. If the idea of getting in at the beginning of something smaller and riding it to the top is of interest to you, then I encourage you to read on. By the time you finish these pages, you'll have a clearer understanding of what Litecoin is, and where it is going.

Through the pages of this book, we hope you will learn a wealth of information that could help you to launch a clear-cut cryptocurrency investment plan with Litecoin.

- What is Litecoin and where did it come from
- What you need to do before you invest in Litecoin
- Investment and Trading tips

- How to get started mining

- How to manage your risks

Many believe that Litecoin is another new and innovative enhancement of the already popular Bitcoin craze. There is a powerful consensus that it is poised to last longer and make even more strides that can change the evolutionary flow of things in the cryptoworld. So, if you hope to start on something really new and exciting and take it as far as it can go, you are ready to start a whole new venture with Litecoin.

There are plenty of books on this subject on the market, thanks again for choosing this one! Every effort was made to ensure it is full of as much useful information as possible. Please enjoy!

Chapter 1: What is Litecoin?

By now, like many others, you've already heard of Bitcoin and how it launched the world into the new cryptocurrency phenomenon. The idea of peer-to-peer transactions was not introduced by cryptocurrency, but it was definitely improved upon. Bitcoin's role was to introduce decentralization to the peer-to-peer transactions, and many of those who got to use it happily lapped it up.

But like all new ideas, no matter how good they are, there are always flaws; little imperfections soon became apparent began to materialize and show that there was a definite need for improvement. It wasn't long before Bitcoin was faced with its own unique set of problems, some of them were simple, and users would happily overlook them but others, like lengthy transaction approval times (mainly as a result of too much congestion) and fees that were just too high, proved to be unacceptable.

The response was a host of developers that went back to the drawing board to see how they could improve the system. The solution finally came from a developer by the name of Charlie Lee who actually used Bitcoin's source code as the foundation for his new currency.

Unlike Bitcoin's mysterious Satoshi Nakamoto, Charlie Lee has always been out front with his ideas about Litecoin. After several failed attempts at a new coin, he finally found success with Litecoin. The new coin was launched in October of 2011 with a combination of source code from Bitcoin and a few other changes to create a coin that would eliminate many of the problems many were experiencing with Bitcoin, and getting rid of some of the bugs that had already killed off several other cryptocurrencies.

It was the way he launched the coin that made it much more secure than Bitcoin or any other cryptocurrencies that preceded it. By releasing the source code prior to the official launch of the coin and encouraging miners to start mining them on Testnet, a platform designed to test new altcoins, he built up anticipation for the coin's release. Before it even made it to the market, people were impressed with the fairness of the system, its speed, and its new Scrypt algorithm. By the time he released his genesis block, its hash rate was so strong that the possibility of an attack was even more difficult than anticipated.

What Makes Litecoin Different from Bitcoin?

Even though he used Bitcoin's source code, Lee made sure that he was not creating an exact clone of the super cryptocoin and made several distinct changes. First was in supply. Rather than limiting supply to a maximum of 21 million coins like Bitcoin, Litecoin was to have 84 million. This was one of the factors that contributed to the speedier transactions times. The more coins to be produced, the smaller the blocks; the smaller the blocks, the faster the transactions.

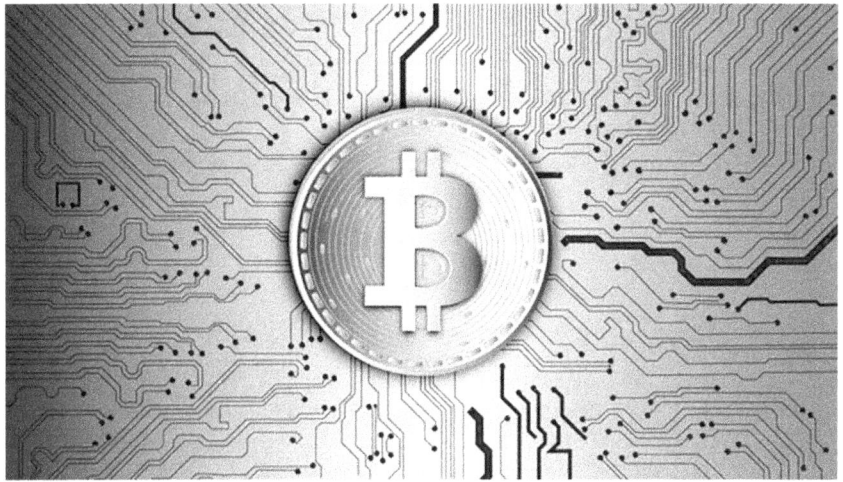

He also changed the consensus algorithm by incorporating the Scrypt proof of work formula to ensure that mining of coins would be more fair.

While Bitcoin's little brother does offer an alternative for users to make payments and purchases across borders, the network uses a number of different mathematical algorithms that allow users to have much more control of their finances. Because of these changes, Litecoin can provide faster confirmation times, better storage capabilities, and it has a great deal more support from the crypto industry, making it a pretty strong contender for taking over Bitcoin at some point in the future. It is now the #5 cryptocurrency on the market.

Like all other cryptocurrencies, it is completely decentralized and operates on the Blockchain. However, Litecoin's Blockchain has many more capabilities than Bitcoin, creating blocks faster, giving its network the ability to support even more transactions than its older brother all without requiring repeated software changes. This factor alone made the coin more appealing to merchants because they could receive faster confirmations and continue to have the option to wait for other confirmations when selling big-ticket items.

Litecoin Mining

There were changes in the way Litecoin is mined as well. Miners could appreciate the new hashing algorithm as well as the number of coins they receive when they have successfully solved a particular block. Once a transaction is made, the data is uploaded to the network where the miners can work to solve the block.

All miners use a unique algorithm to solve the puzzles and create a block. Once the block is completed, the transactions within it are verified to be legitimate and are added to the block. This new system is greatly appreciated as it does not require the purchase of expensive equipment to problems and solve the puzzles. While you do need to have equipment that is compatible with the Litecoin network, unlike Bitcoin, where miners must use costly mining rigs to work out the solutions, miners of Litecoin can use their CPUs or GPUs to do the same thing. Still, anyone interested in mining Litecoins must make sure that the system they have has the exact specifications needed to sync well with their network.

Things That are the Same

One of Litecoin's greatest strengths is its familiarity. While it has made some critical changes that make it stand out from Bitcoin, it is also very similar in form for the user. The benefits to that are clear. Once a merchant begins to accept Bitcoin as payment, it is only a matter of time before they are comfortable with accepting Litecoin as well. This allows the smaller coin to ride Bitcoin's coat tails to the top until it reaches a point where it surpasses Bitcoin and takes the lead itself.

Prospects for the Future

In addition, Litecoin's 6-person development team has lots of plans for the future that would help to propel it past Bitcoin in the future. There is the possibility that as more people build their confidence in Bitcoin, they will use it primarily for more expensive transactions, leaving the microtransaction field wide open for Litecoin to capitalize on.

However, before this is possible, Litecoin still has to overcome one obstacle, the development of a reliable payment processor. Today, Litecoin is going strong and is heading for great heights. If you are interested in taking advantage of this coin before its value soars out of reach, then now is the time to do the necessary research and get set up for an investment.

Chapter 2: Get Your Wallet

Whether you choose to mine, trade, or invest in Litecoin, one of the first things you'll have to do is to obtain your wallet. You can consider your wallet a ticket into the cryptocurrency world. Without it, you cannot perform any transactions, and you have no means of protecting your investment.

You can view your wallet the same way you would view a physical wallet with a few special features added to it. Not only is it a place to store your currency when you receive it, but your digital wallet helps you to keep regular track of all your Litecoins so that you can perform a host of different types of transactions.

- It receives and sends money.

- It can keep a running list of exchanges you trade with.

- It keeps a record of your transaction history.

- And it keeps a watchful eye on your finances.

There is a wide selection of digital wallets each with its own pros and cons. Choosing the right wallet for you will require you to consider several factors. In addition to learning the features of each wallet, you will also have to analyze your personal investment needs and style.

One thing you must always keep in mind is that while cryptocurrency transactions are usually secure, the wallets themselves are often vulnerable. It is important that you understand those vulnerabilities, so you can take the precautionary steps to protect yourself and your assets.

- Most wallets offered on exchanges are maintained and stored in the cloud, which make them vulnerable to hacking and cybercrime.

- Mobile or desktop wallets are stored on your personal computer or mobile device but are vulnerable because they are connected to the Internet where they are subject to cyber thieves, viruses, and malware.

- Paper wallets need to be kept in a secure place where they won't be at risk of environmental dangers or theft.

- Brain wallets are subject to the frailty of the human mind.

In addition, you also have to find out if there are fees for the transactions you plan to make. While some wallets are completely free, others will charge for every move you make. It is up to you to look for hidden fees that they may have. You may make a profit on your investment choices but lose it all in fees that you didn't even know where coming.

Hot and Cold Wallets

While many companies offer wallets for your investment choices, there are two different types you will want to consider. Most people work with at least two, one hot and one cold as their best approach to managing their currency. Hot wallets are those that are connected to the Internet so you can conduct transactions and cold wallets are completely detached and store your information completely offline.

Ideally, it is best to store the bulk of your currency in a cold wallet as it is less vulnerable to illicit activity. Most investors will maintain the majority of the currency in a cold wallet, out of reach of those who might train to steal it and only transfer the amount they wish to invest in the hot wallet. This adds an additional layer of security and protects their funds from unnecessary exposure.

Hardware Wallets

Hardware wallets refer to the hardware that connects to your system. This is usually done through a USB drive that slips right into your additional port. With this type of hardware, you can safely send and receive your coins completely offline. While these types of wallets are great tools for security, they can be rather pricey, so unless you're planning on making some major transactions that will make it worth the additional costs, you might want to look at some other options first.

Of course, it is not enough to understand the features of a wallet to make your decision. It is also important that you know who is backing the software programs that run it. Ideally, you want a company that has a solid and trustworthy reputation. Even if you do not have a lot to invest, it only takes one person to take it all in a matter of seconds.

Today, we know that making transactions with cryptocurrency is secure, but the reality is that every day there are always those who are working very hard to overcome the obstacles that are your security net now. There have been millions of dollars already taken from unsuspecting investors so to avoid scams, always make sure that you go the extra mile to lessen your exposure to scams of all sorts.

Most new investors who are not sure of their outcome, prefer to start out with cheaper wallets until they get their footing in the market. However, the effort you put in to save money may be the very opening that could cause you to lose it. Check out the background of the companies that offer the wallet, the country they are from, the people that offer it, and their track record with past investors.

Tricks Used to Steal Your Coins

It helps to understand the many different tricks people make when it comes to stealing your money.

Keylogging: Hackers can learn your password when you download software from a website that carries the capability of recording all of the keystrokes you make.

Remote Access Control: You may unknowingly download software or an email address that opens a back door so a hacker can gain remote access to your computer. From there they can search your emails and your Litecoins.

Social Engineering: They may attempt to get you to provide information via email, fake websites, or even a phone call pretending that they are someone who is authorized to have such information.

Familiarity: Often thieves are people who actually know you. Maybe not personally, but they have made it their effort to get to know everything about you. The more they learn about you and your personal life, the easier it is to guess your passwords and gain access to your account.

Hackers and all sorts of cyber thieves have one goal in mind; to gain access to the private key that opens the door to your money. Once they have that private key, there is nothing you can do to stop them from accessing your account and cleaning you out.

While there are some who will attempt to take your money by a more direct means, the majority of thieves prefer the anonymity of the Internet. So, the more protected you are from exposure online, the safer your money will be. This is why many investors prefer to place the majority of their funds in a cold wallet and only use those coins that will be actively traded online.

A Word About Exchange Wallets

As a new investor, you will need to set up an account and a wallet with an exchange. This is where your buying and selling will take place. The money you hold in these accounts will definitely be more exposed. So, when you are dealing with the exchange, there are a few guidelines you should follow.

- Make sure that you change your password each time you complete a transaction.

- Only use those exchanges that require two-factor authentication.

- Only keep your money on the exchange for a limited amount of time.

It is easy to see that learning how to deal with cryptocurrency is very different from how we use traditional currency. By taking the necessary precautions, you can at least lower your exposure to theft and keep your Litecoins safe and secure.

What if Something Happens?

While you might be able to avoid threats from scammers and cyber thieves, you can't escape the threat of human imperfection. People inevitably forget their passwords, computers get damaged, and we just might find ourselves in a hurry and accidentally hit the wrong key, deleting all of your records.

The good news is that there are things you can do to recover access to your keys and your address if that happens. Now, this is not a guarantee that you will always be able to do this but at least you will have some recourse you can try so that all may not be lost.

Keep a backup file: One of the first things you want to do is to keep a backup file that contains your keys and your password just in case something does happen. Make sure you don't store it in the same place as your wallet otherwise you could lose that as well. Some wallets even give you the option to sweep or import your address to another device.

You can also create a .dat file that holds both your private and public keys. This way, if your wallet is accidentally deleted all you'd have to do is download it again and move the .dat file to the 'applications' folder.

Finally, you can create a seed key, which can also restore your wallet keys.

These are all useful tips and advice that can help you to protect your coins once you've obtained them, but it is always important to keep in mind that no system is 100% foolproof. Therefore, you should always make sure you do your due diligence and take every precaution to protect your new assets as much as possible. After all, while exchanges and technology promise you protection, the buck really does stop in your court.

Chapter 3: Mining Litecoin

There are many ways you can make money off of Litecoin. Most people automatically fall back to the traditional investment strategy of buying and holding the coins. While this is very profitable, it does have its drawbacks. If you're one of those who has a background in computer programming, processing, and developing, you might find more satisfaction by mining Litecoin.

For most people who are just getting on the cryptocurrency bandwagon, the chance to mine Bitcoin is probably already out of reach. Not only is it cost prohibitive to set up, but with a payout of 12.5 Bitcoins for each block solved, the environment is extremely competitive. However, mining Litecoins offers a very different picture.

Like all cryptocurrencies, no centralized institution manages the flow of money. So when you make a transaction, it is verified and completed by miners. When you place an order for a transaction, it is pooled together with all the other transactions that were created at the same time, encrypted and assembled into blocks.

The miner's job is to create a cryptographic hash that meets a long list of criteria for that block. Using complex mathematical algorithms designed for just that purpose does this. The task is extremely difficult, and the only way to successfully mine a block is to attempt several different methods of computation and continue doing so until you find one that works. This is a time-consuming task, and quite often, another miner solves the block before you can complete the task. When that happens, the only thing to do is to pick up another block and start working on the next one.

While this could be quite frustrating and you could spend a great deal of time working on these algorithms, the reward for successful completion of a mine is currently 25 Litecoins, which depending on the value of the coins at the time could turn out to be a substantial amount of money.

Aside from the challenges of beating the other miners to the solution of the block, there are other drawbacks to mining.

Special Equipment

In the past, when cryptocurrency was first introduced, the task of mining was primarily done with CPUs and later with GPUs, but as more and more people continue to use cryptocurrencies that is rarely the case anymore. Today, most miners have special mining hardware called ASICs, which can work through the mining process many times faster than a normal household computer could. These processors can be quite expensive, and they do not give any guarantee that you will successfully be able to mine a block and earn your Litecoins.

In the meantime, you should understand that they also consume a great deal of power, and as more people join the network as miners, you will be faced with a lot of competition.

Another factor you should bear in mind is that if you are not able to find success as a miner, the equipment you purchase is so very specific to the process that it most likely will have very little resale value except to other miners. In addition, these units are so specific in design that it is virtually impossible for them to be repurposed for another task that you might be interested in.

It is extremely important that you understand all of these drawbacks before you decide you want to try your hand at mining for Litecoin. It is necessary for you to do thorough research and make sure it is a venture you really want to do before you invest in the equipment. However, if you do decide to be a miner, below are a few things you need to do to get set-up.

Acquire Your Software

After you acquire your equipment, you will need to install the software compatible with your system. Litecoin miners use Scrypt as their hashing algorithm. Make sure you have enough memory because the software needed will require a lot of space. Many miners use graphics cards, but don't be fooled; the type of graphics cards that come with your home laptop is not usually sufficient for the kind of work you will demand of it. If you think you'll be able to mine successfully with a home computer, you might find yourself disappointed. It is better to have a dedicated system that will only do mining and nothing else.

If you would rather go a less expensive route, you can use a GPU or a CPU. These will allow you to mine, but it will not work as fast, and you may struggle to keep up with the intensity of the work. Remember, the idea is the faster you mine, the more likely you'll be able to solve a block. Going into mining without the right equipment would be like running a marathon without the right kind of running shoes. You might finish the race, but you'll be far from the head of the pack, no matter how much you prepare. Even those with the right equipment struggle to keep up.

For that reason, many miners try to increase their odds of solving a block by joining a mining pool. A group of miners get together and pool their resources, and work together to solve the blocks. When they do find a solution, they split the returns so that everyone gets a reward.

It can be very rewarding for a miner to solve a block. With a payout of 25 Litecoins for each block solved it is easy to see why so many would rather take a chance. At the time of this writing, a single Litecoin is valued at $189.00, which would earn you a profit of $4,725.00 to let your computer do all the work. If this is the best way to earn money from Litecoin, the method that calls to you, it is very important that you dedicate a good deal of time in researching the equipment and materials needed, evaluate the cost of the power in your area, and seriously consider the process from all angles before you make a final decision

Chapter 4: Trading Litecoin

If mining is not your calling, there are still plenty of other ways you can make money with Litecoin. Some have found a great deal of success from trading instead. There is a definite art to trading any type of cryptocurrency. You not only have to know how to take advantage of the volatility of the market but you also have to understand that at times, you're not just rolling the dice with your own money.

While you can get greater exposure by trading rather than outright investing, you can also experience even greater losses. To create a cushion against potential losses, there are some very basic guidelines you should try to follow. These will help you to avoid making those costly mistakes and know when to get in or out of the market without losing your shirt.

Before we get into it, keep in mind that cryptocurrency trading can be very intense. It is a fast-paced, roller-coaster ride through cryptoland and most people do not have the stomach for it. If after reading this chapter, you feel it is not for you, don't feel bad. This is the reason so many people prefer to do outright investing, which we will discuss in the next chapter. That said, below is a list of basic rules that could save you a lot of sleepless nights if you do decide to try your hand at trading.

- Never enter a trade without a reason. Before you enter into any trade, it is important to do your research and analyze the trends thoroughly. You must have a clear-cut goal in mind and have escape plans in place, in case the trade does not go the way you predicted.

- Know who you're getting in bed with. Many beginners enter the trade thinking with playground rules; everyone is going to play fair. However, in the cryptoworld, this is not always so easy to do. Whales (those who purchase large quantities of currencies in an attempt to push the price up) are always waiting quietly on the sidelines for a newbie to come along. When the price of a coin reaches a point where it can no longer be sustained, they will sell at inflated prices. When the price drops, the new trader is left holding coins that they paid far more than they were really worth. If you were investing, then you could simply hold onto them until the price naturally rose past where you traded for them but not with trading. With some forms of trading, the exchange will close out your trade long before that happens and take your money with it.

- Be willing to stay out. Sometimes, the only way to stay ahead of the game is to not trade at all. When you don't see the numbers going the right way, do not feel compelled to enter a trade in hopes of making a profit. Wait until it is the right time to enter the market, and you'll do much better.

- Always set your stop-loss limits when you enter a trade. It is important to have a clear target in mind in both directions. You must choose a point when you want to cut your losses if the price goes down but also know when to get out of the market on the upside as well.

- Ignore your FOMO (fear of missing out). Watching the charts can be exhilarating when the numbers are what you want to see. They can also be devastating when they aren't. Very few people are happy being spectators on the sidelines so when your FOMO kicks in, let logic take control. Whether it is to get in the game or to get out, you can't let your emotions run the show. Trading is about the numbers, the charts, and the graphs. There is no room for emotional attachment or detachment with any coin, so you'll have to maintain your level of self-control and only make decisions based on the research and analysis you have done.

- Manage your risk. Investors like to stay in the game and squeeze every dime they can out of every investment decision they make, but not so with traders. They look for the small profits and gain their wealth by multiple small movements rather than the big haul many people are looking for.

- Remember Big Brother: People often believe that altcoins are out there standing on their own two feet but in most cases, they are actually riding the coattails of Bitcoin. When Bitcoin is on the rise, usually the altcoins will react. When trading, make sure you don't stray too far from the trends to protect your position.

- Don't forget the fees. This is especially true for the trader since they are often in and out of the market quickly. Traders make trades much more frequently than investors so being hit hard with exchange fees, wallet fees, transfer fees, etc. can easily mount up. Even if you do make a successful trade, you may end up losing money if you don't keep account of the fees you're going to have to pay.

Trading cryptocurrency can be a very fast way to make a lot of money with Litecoin. Whether you're trading your own money or you are margin trading with someone else's you need to know what you're getting into. Remember, this is a zero-sum game, so no matter how much you win in a trade, there is someone on the other end who has lost. For that reason, it is important to never get too comfortable with the idea of a successful trade. Even the best of traders will lose sometimes. With that in mind, your goal is not to be right all the time but to make a profit. So make sure that the profits you do earn are higher than your losses and you will find success in trading Litecoin.

Types of Trading Strategies

Many different strategies can be applied to trading, but the most common are day trading and margin trading. Each of these has their own pros and cons. After reading this next section, you can decide which one will work best for you.

Day Trading: Day trading is exactly as it sounds. It is doing all your trades in a single day. Day traders never go to sleep with their money floating around the exchange. You never know when the price is going to plummet to the floor and you lose everything. No matter what the condition is of the market at the end of the day, a good day trader will collect their winnings and rejoin the party the next morning.

Day trading works best for traders since they are primarily focused on an accumulation of small gains to earn their profits. It is the perfect way to get in and out of the market quickly. However, to be successful at it, you must become very adept at reading charts and graphs, and master the ability to analyze and predict trends. Your success at this strategy will depend largely on how well you can do that. Those that do can earn a great deal of money in a very short amount of time.

Margin Trading: Margin trading involves the use of borrowed money to make the trade. The trader only puts up a percentage of the total amount of an order and the lender (usually the exchange or a broker, puts up the rest. The terms of the trade will depend largely on the agreement made with the lender prior to making the trade.

The goal of the margin trader is to predict the direction of the market. If your predictions are correct, you stand to rake in a huge amount of money in a very short amount of time. However, the risks involved with margin trading can be quite high. If your projections prove to be incorrect, the odds of losing everything are much more real.

Therefore, those who prefer to trade on margin must be prepared to lose with every order they place. While it is important never to invest more than you are prepared to lose, that rule is even more important with margin trading.

You are not alone in this type of venture, and you do not hold all the cards. If you begin to lose on a trade, the exchange house can close the order after your earnings fall to a predetermined point leaving you no opportunity to recoup your losses.

You must have a strong constitution when it comes to margin trading. It can really be a scary ride when you factor in the volatility of cryptocurrencies. It is not the kind of strategy for the faint of heart. However, if you find that you are good at it, you can see some amazing returns in a very short amount of time.

Chapter 5: How to Invest in Litecoin

No doubt about it, Litecoin is a very popular currency and as more people learn about it, is becoming even more appealing. The future looks very bright for Litecoin and probably one of the easiest ways to make money with it is to get in on it early while it is still blossoming. Later, the prices are expected to soar well out of reach for many people.

Investing in Litecoin is remarkably easy. Several strategies can be used; each designed to fit a certain type of investor. Still, it is not without some level of risk so there is a certain amount of research you will need to do before you make any decisions.

There are many differences between trading and investing, but the primary factor that separates traders from investors is how they acquire the coins. Traders speculate on the movement of the coins while investors buy them outright.

The strategies discussed in this chapter will be more in line with understanding the different ways you can actually obtain Litecoins and how to go about it.

Buying Litecoins

By and large, the easiest way to gain possession of Litecoins is to buy them outright. This is usually done through an exchange or a broker. How you plan to pay for these coins will depend largely on the exchange you are working with. All exchanges do not have the same arrangement for purchasing coins. Some will only accept forms of online payments but not cash, others will accept payment through other digital payment formats like Perfect Money or PayPal, and others have arrangements so you can purchase coins in a merchant store or other facility.

Since Litecoin doesn't have the same infrastructure as Bitcoin, you may be limited in your options. For example, nearly every exchange will buy and sell Bitcoin freely, but not all exchanges will accept Litecoin. Those who do accept them may limit how you can pay for them.

Almost every exchange that sells Litecoin will accept fiat currency in some form, and many of them will also allow you to pay for your Litecoins with Bitcoin if you have them.

The exchange you use to purchase may limit your options. For example, if you are in the United States, the field is wide open, and there are quite a few places where you can easily purchase Litecoins, but if you're outside of the country, your options may be restricted. Even if you are a United States citizen, trying to connect to the US via the Internet may be greatly restricted. Trying to purchase through an exchange in another country could also be complicated if they're not open to accepting credits or debits from outside their country.

It is extremely important to do your research before you plan to make a purchase. It bears repeating, not all exchanges offer the same services, accept the same forms of payment, are available to people from all over the globe. Finding one that meets your personal investment criteria may take some time, so do that first. You will save yourself a lot of anxiety and stress if you do.

What to do With Your Coins

What you do with your Litecoins after you have obtained them also requires some careful decision making. There is a wide variety of choices depending on your personal expectations and goals. If you're the kind of investor who is patient and doesn't need to see great returns in the immediate future then the buy and hold strategy is probably the best.

This simply means that after you purchase them, you put them in your cold wallet and let them sit until the price reaches a certain point. Then you sell them and collect your earnings. This is probably the easiest investment strategy you can do as it doesn't require careful monitoring of the price charts, identifying trends, and predicting market movements. Investors simply need to wait until the price is right and then sell.

While there are no guarantees that you will earn a profit with Litecoin, if history is to be the judge, it is a safe bet for this type of strategy. From its inception on, it has proven to be one of the most transparent and definitely one of the most appreciated coins by its community. With a value that rose more than 2000% in 2017, it has a strong promise for the future. If the following years follow the same pattern that Litecoin has consistently held, it is the perfect opportunity for investors to win big with a small coin.

The fact that it is drastically undervalued means that getting in on it now increases your potential for profit. When you compare its current prices with its two counterparts, Bitcoin and Ethereum, you can see clearly that Litecoin is almost destined to come up in the ranks. This positive hope for the future is one of the main reasons why Asian exchanges are embracing it. It has a lower volatility than the other coins, and its innovative technology is right in line with his two brothers.

While the buy and hold strategy is still relatively simple and easy to do, it does not mean that you can sit back on your laurels and do nothing. It is up to you to continuously monitor the movements and statistics. Of course, you won't have to be glued to your computer monitor as you would if you were trading, but part of your protecting your investment is to keep tabs on its growth or losses.

To that end, you should always buy your coins with a specific goal in mind. If you want to wait until it reaches a certain price, then you need to know when that happens. If your goal is to wait until the market cap is at a certain point, then only through your careful monitoring will you be able to accomplish that task. The more you are committed to this part of the investment, the more confident you'll be and the less risk you'll undertake.

Another way to invest is to go short, which basically means that you will not hold your coins for an extended period of time. There could be many reasons why you might choose to go short on your investment choice. This type of investor usually has more time to watch and analyze the market fluctuations and can quickly gauge when the market is ripe for the picking.

While the trends for cryptocurrencies as a whole is upward, if you study the charts daily, you'll quickly notice that they have daily patterns as well. Some coins have fluctuations that can range hundreds of dollars in a single day. If you study these charts for a period of time, you will begin to notice when these fluctuations happen and identify when an uptrend or a downtrend is about to occur.

Going short is very similar to day trading (we discussed in the last chapter) with a small difference. Day traders are in and out of the market in the same day, but short trading can be longer. You could hold your coins for only a few minutes, or you could also hold them for several months. Either way, you only sell them when you know you're going to have a profit.

To that end, again, you must have an end game in mind before you decide to buy. Ask yourself, what is your goal or what do you hope to achieve. This way, you have a clear-cut vision in mind, and you won't be inclined to react to every fluctuation of the market. There is no market more erratic than the cryptocurrency market. Even for stable coins like Litecoin, the fluctuations can be extreme, so it pays to approach this type of investment with a definite plan.

Whether you plan to hold onto your coins for a few seconds or a few months, you need to approach the investment in the same way. By doing thorough research and applying all your intuitive skills, you'll soon be able to anticipate market movements and invest accordingly.

Finally, investing in Litecoin when you are low on funds can be really frightening. Not everyone has enough money on hand to purchase 100 or 1000 coins at a single time. Unlike investing in the stock market, when you choose cryptocurrencies, you are not compelled to shell out large sums of cash to get in on the market. Some investors choose to do something called dollar cost averaging.

This is where you buy only a few coins at frequent intervals. With dollar cost averaging, you take the total amount of your planned investment and divide it up over equal time periods, buying your coins a little at a time. You can do this indefinitely, or you can have a set time limit when you want the payments to cease.

If you have a credit card, you could set it up as an automatic payment in the same way that you set up automatic payments for your car or your home. This way, it becomes a part of your regular budget, and you won't even have to think about it.

There are a lot of advantages to using dollar cost averaging. First, it provides a buffer for those times when the prices are extremely high. Because you're not purchasing a large quantity of coins at a single time, the price is averaged out over an extended period of time actually cushioning you from major losses.

With dollar cost averaging, the amount you invest remains the same at every interval, but since the price will vary each time you make a purchase, there will be some periods where you purchase more coins than others. This system works best in combination with the buy and hold strategy as the profits you earn will compound over an extended period of time.

Dollar cost averaging makes it possible for more people to get in on the market without having to expend thousands of dollars they don't have. If you're low on cash but still want to take advantage of the potential that Litecoin has to offer, this is the best way to do it. In addition, since right now Litecoin is undervalued, the expectation is that it will rise quickly and before long it may be completely out of reach for many people. There is no reason to hesitate when it comes to buying Litecoins because this strategy makes it possible for everyone to have a chance at big profits with cryptocurrency.

Reasons for Investing

It doesn't matter if you want to invest or trade; regardless of your decision, you should have a reason for making the decision. Of course, your reason is you want to make money, but to get involved in something as volatile as cryptocurrency, you should think deeper than that. In fact, it is your reasoning that will help you to develop your own personal investment plan; it might even be the deciding factor as to which investment strategy you will take.

Without having thought this process through, you could open yourself up to some very costly mistakes and end up losing all of your Litecoins. This is especially true for the beginning investor. So, we are going to list a few factors that can help you to determine why you have chosen Litecoin and how that can help you to strategize an investment plan that will suit you best.

What is Your Why?

Every major decision in your life needs to address this question. Whether you're planning on investing for a short time or you plan on making this a career choice, the *why* is very important. As we said before, this is a zero-sum game, so someone is always going to lose, no matter what happens. No one will win at this all the time, so you must be aware that there will be times when you can fully expect to lose so to make it worth your while, determine your why.

Decide on a Stop-Loss

It might be easy to decide to buy in and just wait to see what the market will do. Sell when it feels like you've earned enough. That is a common mistake that many newbies do. They don't have a clear-cut plan on when to exit the market. The result is that they stay for a little too long and they cut their profits as a result.

By setting your stop-loss before you enter the trade, you are making sure that you don't get emotionally attached to the investment and linger too long. When things begin to go south, it is easy to hope for the best, thinking that things will turn around and you'll be back on top. This might work well for those who choose to buy and hold their coins, but with any other strategy, it could signal the beginning of the end.

Control Your FOMO

Newcomers often get the investment bug. They get a taste of how easy it is to make money and are compelled to get in on every possible buy-in they see. When the prices look good, the urge to buy can be very strong, but sometimes it is better to sit back and wait to see what is really happening. We've already talked about the whales, those who buy up a lot of currency, pushing the price upward and giving a false impression of its true value. If you were to buy in at the top of this peak, it could be a long time before you're able to recover that deficit, if ever. Wise investors are patient and observe the market carefully before they decide to buy.

Manage Your Risk

Never invest more than you can afford to lose. As a matter of fact, one expert actually advised newbies to view the money they put into an investment as already lost. If you earn a profit, then that's all the better, but if you lose you won't be disappointed. The more you manage your risk level, limit your exposure to unnecessary losses, and know what you can afford, the better your chances of success will be.

Research

There is nothing more important to your success as an investor than research. The more you learn about the market before you begin, the lower your risk is. Even though the market is extremely new, there is already so much to learn that you may never master it all. It is also an evolving market, going through changes at every turn. If you really want to be a successful investor, you won't stop at reading these pages. You'll keep up with financial reports, news items, social media comments, and the countless forums as they talk about the different movements of the prices and what they mean. The more information you know, the easier it will be to get started with confidence. Something you'll need as you start down this exciting path to new money.

Just as a reminder, here are a few tips that will help you to get started on the right foot:

- Do a strategic analysis to find the right exchange to use.

- Do a feasibility analysis to make sure that Litecoin is the right choice for you.

- Determine what resources you can afford to invest.

- Determine how much you can afford to lose (this involves more than money, you must also factor in the amount of time you have to monitor its growth, and how much of your energy you're willing to spend)

- Prepare yourself mentally. Remove the emotion from the investment and focus on the logic behind it.

- Determine the best strategy to use.

- Create a financial plan. This means thinking about your resources, your current financial situation, your tolerance for risk, and your goals for the future.

Know Your Risks

There are many reasons to invest in Litecoin, some you probably already are aware of, but that doesn't mean there are no risks. You should be very familiar with the ways things could also turn bad when investing in Litecoin.

- Hacking: because Litecoin is a digital currency, it only exists in the digital world. You can only spend it online, buy it online, and sell it online. For that reason, anytime you are connected to the Internet or on a system that can tap into your storage, there is a risk of hacking. You might think that trusting a third party system to manage your money is wise but keep in mind, these companies that offer to hold your currency for you are not banks, which are bound by law to protect your assets. You may get some assistance if your coins are lost or stolen but don't expect too much. It is up to you to protect yourself from hackers.

- Regulation: Another risk you might face is the lack of regulation. Unlike banks and other financial institutions, cryptocurrencies have yet to have the tight regulations that can protect you. You will not earn interest on your investment, so the only way you can earn anything is with an increase in price. If the price drops, you lose. There are no regulations as of yet, to prevent major losses if they should occur.

- Scammers: Never follow rumors without verifying the information you hear. The percentage of frauds and scams in cryptocurrency is extremely high. Always make sure that you know exactly what you're investing in and have checked them out thoroughly. These are not companies with a CEO at the helm, so there is no one to contact if you are defrauded.

- Privacy: While transactions with cryptocurrency are always private, what may not be private is your connection with your exchange. Many exchanges require you to provide a lot of personal information to open an account. So, if you're uncomfortable with that information being held on an exchange, then you'll have to do additional research to find exchanges that will allow anonymous buys and sells. There are not many, but there are a few that will allow purchases in cash without having to present identification.

- Transactions are permanent: This cannot be stressed enough. Once you make a transaction with a cryptocurrency, it can't be reversed. It is of the utmost importance that you don't make a mistake. Transposing numbers, using the wrong key, or just hitting the wrong key could cause you to unwittingly send your money to the wrong person. If that happens, there is no way to get it back. There is no way to retrieve lost funds so it is up to you to make sure that you're dealing with a legitimate merchant or customer and that you do everything exactly as it should be. Cryptocurrency is an unforgiving world, and you could lose everything with just a single mistake.

- It's a volatile market: The price of coins fluctuates wildly. If you've watched leaders of the pack, like Bitcoin or Ethereum, you'll notice that a price could move as much as a thousand dollars, sometimes more, in a single day. Cryptocurrency prices are not supported by any government, so their value is determined purely by supply and demand. With a market cap on the creation of new Litecoins, this along with a lack of regulations, it is no telling where the prices could go. Some have already learned how to manipulate the market in ways that could harm your investment.

It might sound exciting to win big with Litecoin or any other cryptocurrency, but it does involve work. More than many might realize. If you're new to investing, you're probably thinking like most, that it is just buying and waiting, which is only true in some of the cases but definitely not all. By having some basic guidelines and rules to follow you can keep your feet pointed in the right direction, and you can focus your energies where they can benefit you best without letting yourself get carried away by all of the exciting talk and big promises you are destined to

hear.

Chapter 6: How to Choose an Exchange

Throughout this book, we've discussed several strategies on how to invest in Litecoin. There is one more feature that we must cover before you're ready. That is how to choose an exchange through which you will buy your Litecoins.

As you begin your research, you'll quickly notice that there are quite a few exchanges to choose from. As a new trader, it could seem overwhelming to go through all the options before you, but it is important that you choose your exchange carefully. There are a few key points you can look for that can help you to narrow down your decision.

- Does it trade Litecoin? Not all exchanges accept all cryptocurrencies. In this world, there is no such thing as a one-stop shop where you can pick and choose which currencies you want to buy. Some exchanges will offer some coins while others will not. You may have to shop around to find the exchange that has Litecoin on the menu. The good news is that because Litecoin is one of the top five currencies available today, there are a lot more exchanges that offer it than some of the other lesser-known currencies.

- Get the exchanges background. The more information you know about the exchange, the easier it will be to decide if it will make a good partner for you. When you're gathering this information, don't just accept what's written on the first page of their website, but be willing to dig a little deeper. Important information to have is the name of the founder, its location, the kind of trading it does, the traffic, etc. If you find you're having difficulty locating this kind of information, it might be best to stay away from that one and search out one that is more forthcoming.

- Governance is also very important. Some exchanges are located in other countries outside of the United States so they will not have the same regulations. In some cases, there aren't any regulations to speak of. Whatever the case, you need to know what their responsibility is to you and what you can expect from them.

- Security protocols. Every exchange has different security measures, so you want to be sure that they are going to do everything in their power to keep your identity (if they require it) and your assets safe. Look for exchanges that require two-factor authentication to be absolutely sure that you can communicate with them if you need to.

- Ease of use. When you are new to investing, it can be confusing to navigate through the dashboard of some exchanges. Many do not give enough guidance to newbies so to take the frustration out of your experience, find one that makes it easy for you to get started.

- What other currencies do they offer: You may not want to stop at Litecoin. If you plan on investing in other currencies, then it would be easier to do so if you choose an exchange that offers multiple coins so you can handle all your business in one location.

- Fees. One thing that many new investors constantly overlook are the fees. Some exchanges demand fees for every little move you make while others require very little. Often it is the fees that can make or break a profit so make sure you know what you're going to have to pay to complete your investment.

- Customer Support: It is also very important to check out their customer support. We all want to know that we can get assistance when we need it. Having a person you can chat with, one that speaks your language, is knowledgeable, and capable can be a godsend when you're struggling with something.

- Finally, you want to know what payment options they accept: You'd be surprised how many different payment options are now available, especially since the advent of cryptocurrencies. If you're transferring your money from a bank or other financial institution, you may not have a problem, but if you're planning to pay with a credit or debit card, PayPal, Skrill or some other money exchange system, you might be surprised at the complications you will face. Some of these exchanges require a lot of detailed information before you can open your account. It would be very frustrating to go through that entire process only to find that they will not accept your preferred payment option.

Choosing an exchange for your investment playground is just as important as choosing the right wallet to store your currency. It may take time to shop around for the right match, but when you do, the rewards will be immense. The more care you take in these decisions, the better your chances of having a wonderful experience when you start investing in Litecoin.

Conclusion

Thank you for making it through to the end of *Litecoin: Best Strategies for Investing and Profiting From Litecoin*, let's hope it was informative and able to provide you with all of the tools you need to achieve your goals whatever it may be.

We've finally reached the end of our journey. By now, you've learned a lot about how to invest in Litecoin. Of course, you haven't learned everything, but we hope that you've learned enough to get started on the right foot. It might seem overwhelming at first, but in time, you'll soon discover that you'll be able to navigate the system like a pro.

Litecoin is a cryptocurrency that is grossly undervalued, and this is the perfect time to enter into this type of investment. Right now, the prices are low, but as the world begins to become more familiar with the power of this little coin, the demand will increase and so will its price. However, armed with the right information, it can become a powerful investment tool that could earn you a lot of money.

If you are seriously thinking about investing in Litecoin, you're on the right track. It is an intelligent move that could allow you to enter the growing cryptocurrency market at the beginning of something big and allow your investment to grow with it.

Through the pages of this book, you've learned about:

- What Litecoin is and a little of its history

- What you need to get set up to invest in Litecoin

- Simple strategies for trading Litecoin

- Simple investment strategies

- How to manage your level of risk

- How to choose a wallet and an exchange

We hope that your interest has been peaked to learn more about this wonderful cryptocurrency and how you can make it a part of your future investment plans. If we have succeeded, then we'll see you on the platform, hopefully raking in the dough with amazing success.

Happy Investing!

Finally, if you found this book useful in anyway, a review on Amazon is always appreciated!